DI.

DATE DUE

A scene from the Vineyard Theatre production of *Unwrap Your Candy*.

Photo by Carol Rosegg

UNWRAP
YOUR CANDY

AN EVENING OF ONE-ACT PLAYS

BY DOUG WRIGHT

★

DRAMATISTS
PLAY SERVICE
INC.

★

UNWRAP YOUR CANDY
Copyright © 2002, Doug Wright

All Rights Reserved

UNWRAP YOUR CANDY received its world premiere at the Vineyard Theatre (Douglas Aibel, Artistic Director) in New York city on October 8, 2001. The casts were as follows:

1. UNWRAP YOUR CANDY

THE PHYSICIAN .... Reg Rogers
THE FASHIONABLE WOMAN .... Leslie Lyles
THE GABBY LADY .... Michi Barall
THE WELL-DRESSED MAN .... Henry Stram
THE NARCOLEPTIC .... Darren Pettie

2. LOT 13: THE BONE VIOLIN

THE AUCTIONEER .... Reg Rogers
THE MOTHER .... Leslie Lyles
THE FATHER .... Darren Pettie
THE DOCTOR .... Michi Barall
THE PROFESSOR .... Henry Stram

3. WILDWOOD PARK

MS. HAVILAND .... Leslie Lyles
DR. SIMIAN .... Reg Rogers

4. BABY TALK

THE PSYCHIATRIST .... Henry Stram
THE HUSBAND .... Reg Rogers
ALICE .... Michi Barall
THE BABY .... Darren Pettie

WILDWOOD PARK and BABY TALK were commissioned by McCarter Theatre, Princeton, New Jersey. Earlier versions of the following three plays were originally produced by McCarter Theatre. The casts were as follows:

LOT 13: THE BONE VIOLIN

THE AUCTIONEER .... Jonathan Walker
THE MOTHER .... Olivia Birkelund
THE FATHER .... Tom Nelis
THE PROFESSOR .... Jefferson Mays
THE DOCTOR .... Joanna P. Adler

WILDWOOD PARK

MR. HAVILAND .... Olivia Birkelund
DR. SIMIAN .... Jonathan Walker

BABY TALK

THE PSYCHIATRIST .... Jefferson Mays
THE HUSBAND .... Jonathan Walker
ALICE .... Joanna P. Adler
BABY .... Tom Nelis

UNWRAP YOUR CANDY
A Curtain-Raiser — Part One

CHARACTERS

THE ANNOUNCER

THE PHYSICIAN

THE FASHIONABLE WOMAN

THE GABBY LADY

THE WELL-DRESSED MAN

THE NARCOLEPTIC

SETTING

The play may be performed in the actual house of the theater, or in a bank of theater seats onstage which confront the audience like a fun-house mirror.

NOTE

All of the voices are taped, with the exception of the Gabby Lady, who performs her lines live.

UNWRAP YOUR CANDY
A Curtain-Raiser — Part One

The house lights dim to half, and an announcer speaks over a public address system.

ANNOUNCER. Good evening, ladies and gentlemen, and welcome to the *(Insert name of theater producing this play.)* We'd like to remind you that flash photography and sound recording of any kind is strictly forbidden. Please take a moment to turn off all beepers, cell phones and pagers at this time. *(Lights rise on a set of theater seats identical to those in the house. It's as if the audience is staring at itself in a fun-house mirror. A physician — ticket stub in hand — locates his onstage seat. As he settles — arranging his coat, holding his playbill in his mouth — there is nothing extraordinary or unusual about his manner. However — as he gets comfortable — we hear his thoughts:)*
PHYSICIAN. I should turn off my beeper, I really should. There's no reason not to; the surgery went well. Thank God for my hands; the dexterity of a Van Cliburn. A Swiss clockmaker. And stitching him up afterward ... it was *art.* It was *petit point.* So why should they beep? They won't beep. *(An edge of doubt seeps into his voice.)* If only there hadn't been that confusion with the charts ... goddamn nurses. So careless. Of course it was Mr. Waldman, it had to be, you saw him yourself before surgery ... a pan-procto colectomy and ileostomy ... you went over the procedure, painstakingly, incision by incision. He signed the consent forms, even made a little joke. *(With panic dawning.)* But did he have a goatee? I don't remember. The guy on the table — the fellow we strapped down — *I'll be damned if he didn't have a beard — (Lights out on the physician. The announcer continues:)*
ANNOUNCER. If you've brought any hard candies or cough drops you intend to enjoy during the performance please unwrap

them now. *(Lights rise on a Fashionable Woman a few seats away from the Physician. She, too, behaves with utter normalcy. But as she slips her purse beneath her seat, we hear her thoughts as well:)*

FASHIONABLE WOMAN. It's not directed at me. Not me *specifically.* It just feels that way. How can they know I'm hypoglycemic? That I have a pre-existing medical condition? Of course I've brought candy. And if my blood sugar drops, I'll have to make a dive for it. But no one will notice. I know exactly where they are. The bottom left-hand corner of my purse, behind my car keys, next to my thumb cymbals and my castanets. Besides, what's the alternative? I get psychotic when I ignore the warning signs. God, that time in the Milwaukee Airport, when I rode round and round on the luggage carousel, screaming for sex. If only I'd had a mint! A piece of chewing gum! Thank God for that baggage handler. He was so patient. So obliging. Oh, and that incident with the Clinique girl at Bergdorf's. Hiring that lawyer. All her medical bills. Thank God she got her eyesight back. *(The woman shudders.)* For Christ's sake, what's the lesser evil? *Crinkling a candy-wrapper, or assault and battery? (She rummages in her purse. The sound of a million crash-boxes tumbling over in a heap. Surrounding cast members glare at her. She unwraps a candy — crinkling as loud as air-raid sirens — then notices that she is under incriminating scrutiny. Chastened, she sets her purse down. Lights out on the Fashionable Woman. Lights rise on a Gabby Lady, seated next to the physician. Her cell phone rings. She answers it.)*

GABBY LADY. *(Live, on the telephone.)* Oh, hi … No, I'm at the theater. THE THEATER. I don't know what it is, we have a subscription, I hear it's short … You're having a WHAT? A HYSTERECTOMY? Really? Oh, Helen, relax. I wouldn't tell anyone about that, that's private … *(Lights rise on a Well-Dressed Man, glancing at the Gabby Lady.)*

WELL-DRESSED MAN. Christ, just my luck. That woman's a talker. A chatterbox with no "off switch"; white noise passing as a person. *(Imitating her:)* "What did he say?" "She looks taller on film." "Is it over?" Here we sit, two hundred people in the dark, willing her to die. But does she care? Does she give a rat's ass? No, Old Flip-Lips just keeps chattering away, blithely blathering, oblivious. *My God, you people. (The voice in his brain shouts:)* STAY HOME. STAY HOME AND TALK BACK TO REGIS, FOR CHRISSAKES.

TALK BACK TO JAY FUCKING LENO. *(He notices the Fashionable Woman, who is struggling with the volume dial on an infrared headset.)* Oh, Christ. *An infrared headset. (Imitating the feedback from the headset.)* PHHHFFFFF ... beep, beep ... "To be or not to be" ... PHHHHFFFF. *(Hissing at the oblivious Fashionable Woman:)* Honestly, you deaf cow, you should learn to read lips. Go to art museums instead. Just look at things. *(His attention returns to the talker in front of him. He stares at her with laser-like intensity:)* What if ... I were to reach out ... take an ear in each hand ... and yank them back — quickly — so her eyeballs popped clean out of their sockets ... *(He leans into the Gabby Lady, and asks politely:)* Pardon me? Would you mind speaking a tad more softly?

GABBY LADY. Sure, no problem. *(Into the telephone:)* Helen, I have to go. There's a fucking Nazi sitting behind me. *(Lights rise on a Narcoleptic, snoring away. Sawing wood. A real foghorn, this guy. Suddenly, he bolts awake in his seat.)*

NARCOLEPTIC. Was that me? Did I snore? Christ, did I drool? God, these seats are awful. The back really cuts into your spine, and the arms are so thin ... *(Insert name of rival theater here.)*, now they have great seats. Plush. With those little plaques. Plenty of space to kick back, catch some z's. 'Course, they're upscale, you pay more ... but God, those seats, they're ... dreamland ... they're *Posturepedic* ... next year, it's *(Rival theater.)*, no question ... *(The Physician's beeper goes off. He checks it, and his face fills with anxiety. Cell phones start to ring like car alarms. Beepers trill. Candy wrappers crinkle at deafening levels. Snores like air raid sirens. Monumental sighs. People creak and shift in their seats with seismic force. We even hear gastrointestinal rumblings from sated, well-fed patrons. the entire audience is a cacophony of sound. The announcer finishes, shouting into a bullhorn over the maddening din:)*

ANNOUNCER. NOW SIT BACK!!! RELAX!!! AND ENJOY THE SHOW!!! *(The Physician, the Fashionable Woman, the Well-Dressed Man, the Gabby Lady and the Narcoleptic all glance heavenward, as if the announcer were none other than the voice of God. Chastened, they fall into a silent hush. They peer out at the actual audience, rapt now, eager for the show to begin.)*

End of Part One

LOT 13: THE BONE VIOLIN
A Fugue for Five Actors

CHARACTERS

THE AUCTIONEER — A no-nonsense professional.

THE MOTHER — A well-meaning woman overwhelmed by the enormity of life.

THE FATHER — Pragmatic. Earthbound. "No Frills."

THE DOCTOR — A bespectacled woman in a lab coat. Aryan.

THE PROFESSOR — Supercilious, with discontent born of thwarted ambitions.

SETTING

Downstage sits a table, about six feet in length, covered by a linen cloth. Further upstage are four stools with corresponding music stands. Stage left, a podium.

LOT 13: THE BONE VIOLIN
A Fugue for Five Actors

*In the distance, the sound of an orchestra tuning, and the
busy hum of an audience settling before a concert. The
Mother, The Father, The Professor and The Doctor all enter
and approach their respective music stands. Each begins to
"tune up"; staccato consonants, nonsense words, perhaps even
a few dissonant scales. The Auctioneer enters and takes his
place behind the podium. He nods at the assembled four.
They instantly quiet and give him a courteous nod, as if he
were, say, a musical conductor and not an auctioneer at all.
He slams his gavel and announces in a loud voice:*

THE AUCTIONEER.   LOT THIRTEEN. *(The four other
characters speak rapidly, their words trailing in and out of another,
creating a kind of vocal symphony. Most of the time, they address
the audience directly. Occasionally, they speak among themselves. A
few times, they reenact snippets of dialogue from the past.)*
THE MOTHER. I never wanted to play the violin. I don't even
like classical music.
THE FATHER. The Stones. Led Zeppelin. To me, that's classic.
THE MOTHER.   Psychologists say we're always thrusting our
dreams onto the shoulders of our children. Well, I wanted to be a
dog groomer.
THE DOCTOR. Nature or nurture?
THE MOTHER. No lie. A dog groomer.
THE DOCTOR. The chicken or the egg?
THE MOTHER. You dream bigger for your kids.
THE DOCTOR. The zygote, or Choate?
THE MOTHER. I went to a genealogist once. He said one of my

ancestors had been a harpsichordist. In Prague.

THE FATHER. Went back eight generations, just to come up with that.

THE DOCTOR. Ph.D …

THE MOTHER. If we were religious, we'd call it a gift from God.

THE DOCTOR. … or DNA?

THE MOTHER. When he was born, the first thing I noticed: his hands.

THE DOCTOR. The ovum, or the Ivy League?

THE MOTHER. Such elegant fingers for a baby.

THE DOCTOR. Molecules, or Montessori? Tanglewood or testes?

THE FATHER. He'd wrap those little mitts around my thumb, and I knew he wasn't going to wind up laying bricks.

THE DOCTOR. *Well…?*

THE MOTHER. It all started in nursery school, during Music Corner. *(A few, plucky notes sound in the still air, which The Mother identifies:)* Peter and the Wolf.

THE FATHER. Kid hummed it in the tub.

THE MOTHER. In his sleep.

THE FATHER. With his mouth full.

THE MOTHER. By his fourth birthday, he was hounding us for a violin.

THE FATHER. I bought him a baseball bat instead.

THE MOTHER. A mother expects certain milestones. Tying shoelaces. Scissors. But *this?*

THE FATHER. He took his pocket knife, and his brand-new Louisville slugger … the kid started whittling.

THE MOTHER. There were wood chips all over his dungarees.

THE FATHER. Until …

THE MOTHER and THE FATHER. *(In unison.) Voilà!*

THE MOTHER. He'd carved a perfect *bow.*

THE FATHER. So much for Babe Ruth.

THE MOTHER. He stole his father's tennis racket. Stripped the frame and re-strung it with fishing line. *(Again, a few notes from* Peter and the Wolf, *but this time with a distinctly atonal, improvised feel.)*

THE MOTHER. *(Marveling.)* A homemade violin.

THE FATHER. We shoulda known then.

THE MOTHER. He had this remarkable gift for — what would

you call it?

THE PROFESSOR. *(Drily:)* Transformation. *(Everyone regards the Professor for a beat. The Mother pauses, then opts to continue.)*

THE MOTHER. He'd go out back, to the old Chevy.

THE FATHER. It's on cinder blocks.

THE MOTHER. He'd sit in that car for hours.

THE FATHER. Scrap mostly, but the radio works.

THE MOTHER. Listening. Tune after tune.

THE FATHER. Only had to hear 'em once.

THE MOTHER. And he could play them right back.

THE FATHER. The kid was Memorex.

THE MOTHER. Note for note.

THE FATHER. Eerie.

THE MOTHER. I read Alice Miller. Ignore a child's creativity, and he'll grow up lopsided. Encourage it, and he slices off his ear, or drowns himself.

THE FATHER. It's a no-win situation.

THE MOTHER. Suppose you were in your garden, pulling weeds. Suppose for the first time, you noticed a beautiful rhododendron growing up through the crabgrass. You'd water it, wouldn't you?

THE PROFESSOR. "Natural abilities are like natural plants; they need pruning by study." Sir Francis Bacon.

THE MOTHER. We found this college instructor. In town.

THE PROFESSOR. My last tutorial had ended badly. A tiny princess with a monstrous cello between her knees. Her parents made accusations so sinister and baroque I began to question their proclivities, never mind my own.

THE MOTHER. At first, he was skeptical.

THE PROFESSOR. I'd been an early bloomer myself. At twelve, you're a marvel. At thirty, you're lucky to be playing in summer bandshells. The score to *Gigi*. The best of Barry Manilow. Or, if you've a modicum of cleverness left over from your all-too distinguished adolescence … you teach.

THE MOTHER. Still, he agreed to audition our mini concert master.

THE PROFESSOR. In strode a small boy, balancing a horrific instrument under his chin — all tennis string, and jagged wood. I handed him a few sheets of Strauss.

15

THE MOTHER. "Oh, he can't read music. He plays by ear."

THE PROFESSOR. I cringed. And then he lifted his bow. Two distinct versions of Beethoven's *Sonata Number Eight*. I recognized them both. The first — *(We hear a few bars of the* Sonata, *which The Professor immediately pinpoints:)* — was Zukerman's, an Angel recording circa 1974.* The second — *(Again, we hear a few bars of the* Sonata, *this time with increased vibrato.)* — was Isaac Stern's, performing with the Berliner Philharmoniker, Philips, 1986.* The boy duplicated them with unerring accuracy; each tremor, each trill. He would soon play a third and superior rendition. His own. *(The professor listens silently for a moment, closing his eyes in rapture.)*

THE MOTHER. The professor was so *impressed*.

THE PROFESSOR. I know how Pope Julius felt when Michelangelo unveiled the Sistine ceiling. I know, because that's how I felt the first time I heard him play.

THE MOTHER. He offered a *very* generous scholarship.

THE PROFESSOR. My first violin was an Amati, bequeathed to me by my Italian grandfather. I, in turn, gave it to my new protégé.

THE FATHER. The kid had one thing in his favor. He wasn't Japanese.

THE PROFESSOR. At five, he'd mastered Beethoven and Bruch. At six, he could perform Sarasate's *Zigeunerweisen*. Blindfolded. At seven, he was taxing my abilities as a teacher. As he played velvet phrase after velvet phrase, I'd doodle nervously on his sheet music, then offer some innocuous critique. I prayed that my feeble words wouldn't impugn his natural instincts.

THE MOTHER. If driving two hours three times a week to the university is a crime ...

THE PROFESSOR. He should've moved on.

THE MOTHER. If taking my child to his music lessons is an act of malice ...

THE PROFESSOR. A mentor worthy of his staggering gifts.

THE MOTHER. Go ahead.

THE PROFESSOR. But I was addicted.

THE MOTHER. String me up.

THE FATHER. Prof said our kid was a regular Perlman.

THE PROFESSOR. To him, I was vestigial. To me, he was the Grail.

---

* See Special Note on Songs and Recordings on copyright page.

THE FATHER. Who the hell's Perlman?

THE PROFESSOR. I was flying to New York for a music conference. I took the child to perform for a team of colleagues. Tchaikovsky's *Melancholique. (It fills the room.)* Every note — the plaintive sadness soaring into despair, the lilting cry of a broken heart — poured forth with volcanic force from the body of a seven-year-old boy. I stood in the wings, reduced to tears. *(The music concludes.)* As he left the stage, he turned to me. "My bubble gum," he said, "Give it back." I uncurled my fist, and he popped the pink wad into his mouth. I didn't know whether to embrace or throttle him.

THE FATHER. A man should support his children, not the other way around. But the carpooling, the tuxedo fittings, the concert tours ...

THE MOTHER. I couldn't do it alone.

THE FATHER. I let the day job go.

THE MOTHER. At the supermarket, I'd hear the other mothers whispering, " ... robbed of a normal childhood ... " People tend to say that of children with certain ... well ... advantages.

THE FATHER. I grew up normal. Look where it got me.

THE PROFESSOR. The artist is a willing casualty.

THE FATHER. A back-breakin' mortgage. Bifocals. Chronic gas pains.

THE MOTHER. *(Under her breath, to her husband.)* Shh.

THE PROFESSOR. His sacrifices as well as his skills catapult him beyond mere martyrdom into the realm of the divine.

THE FATHER. You can keep "normal."

THE MOTHER. When Dick hits a home run or Jane sells the most cookies, those are achievements, too. They're just not worthy of the world's attention, that's all.

THE PROFESSOR. We toured for months. Venice. Düsseldorf.

THE MOTHER. I never dreamed I'd see Salzburg.

THE FATHER. We coulda planned a vacation. Put a little back each month.

THE MOTHER. I never knew I wanted to go, until I'd already been.

THE PROFESSOR. Soon, the parasites descended.

THE FATHER. I met Sting backstage at *The Tonight Show.* And we got a two page layout in *Time.*

THE MOTHER. And that high-powered doctor.

THE DOCTOR. Is talent acquired … or is it bred in the bone?

THE MOTHER. All those frozen test tubes.

THE DOCTOR. I first posed that question in an article entitled "Grafting the Muse," *Genetic Engineering Journal*, September 1994.

THE FATHER. All those I.Q. tests we had to take.

THE DOCTOR. Now I'm not one of those fanatics up in Cambridge who believe amino acids code our taste in wallpaper, and carry the names of our grandchildren. Environment plays a part. Still, the root of who we are … our potential … that's imbedded.

THE FATHER. "The Institute for Genetic Predetermination."

THE DOCTOR. Highly misunderstood. "Master Race, neo-Nazi." We get that all the time.

THE FATHER. Some blue-ribbon sperm bank.

THE DOCTOR. I won't pretend our selection process is democratic. It's highly elitist, no question. But what the public fails to recognize — what they fail to admit, in their collective egoism — is that a born biophysicist benefits us all. A born Tolstoy benefits us all. And these people *can* be born.

THE MOTHER. Imagine. Designer children.

THE DOCTOR. What we needed was proof, on a grand scale. A scientific milestone with show-biz appeal.

THE FATHER. Three Nobel prize winners in the fridge, and they wanted our kid, too.

THE DOCTOR. Inside that boy's body swam countless incipient Mozarts. We were confident that, with him on our team, we could breed an entire orchestra.

THE FATHER. Hell, I was flattered.

THE MOTHER. He was more than a child. He was … my baby was …

THE DOCTOR. The necessary clue.

THE PROFESSOR. A pint-sized virtuoso with gargantuan coat-tails.

THE FATHER. A chip off some bigger, better block.

THE MOTHER. No. No. A miracle. He was a *miracle. (A beat.)*

THE DOCTOR. We sanitized a vial, sat back, and waited for the onset of pubescence. *(They wait. The tick-tock of a clock as seconds pass. Then minutes. Finally:)* The donation never occurred. *(There*

18

is a brief pause. The professor tips his head toward the Auctioneer.)

THE PROFESSOR. *(To the Auctioneer:)* Psst. *(The Professor tips his head toward the downstage table.)*

THE MOTHER. Is it time for that? Already?

THE FATHER. Must be. *(The Auctioneer crosses to the table and pulls off the linen cloth with a flourish, revealing a small mahogany coffin, about four feet in length. He returns to the podium. He pounds his gavel a second time.)*

THE AUCTIONEER. PAGE NUMBER SEVEN IN YOUR CATALOGUE. *(Another brief rest.)*

THE FATHER. Kid never saw his tenth birthday.

THE DOCTOR. When we lost him, we lost funding.

THE FATHER. Had a bicycle in the garage, waiting.

THE MOTHER. His hands.

THE FATHER. Blue bicycle.

THE MOTHER. I'll always remember his hands.

THE FATHER. With a horn.

THE DOCTOR. One day, you're the darling of the Fords, the Mellons, the MacArthurs. The next day, you're staging phone-a-thons. Auctions. Even the occasional car wash.

THE MOTHER. I wished I'd never heard the name Riccardo Muti.

THE PROFESSOR. I'd met Maestro Muti only once before, at the London Academy. We weren't formally *introduced*, but we did exchange words. Rub shoulders. Rumor has it he was in the room. And now he was requesting to perform with my prize pupil. *(The Mother pulls out a small concert program.)*

THE MOTHER. I kept the program.

THE PROFESSOR. Together, Muti and I would ruminate over every measure of music.

THE MOTHER. Still crisp. Unopened.

THE PROFESSOR. We'd dissect each piece with the same care and intensity a bomb technician employs when detonating explosives. *(The Mother reads from the program:)*

THE MOTHER. "Paganini. Concerto Number One. The Philadelphia Orchestra."

THE PROFESSOR. "Maestro," I'd offer, "perhaps we should conclude the evening with the *Perpetuum Mobile*." "Please," he'd respond, "Call me Riccardo."

THE FATHER. Rehearsing the *Rondo*. That's when the kid cracked.

THE MOTHER. Perhaps it was exhaustion.

THE FATHER. Perhaps it was nerves.

THE DOCTOR. Perhaps it was a failed synapse.

THE PROFESSOR. Perhaps it was his own angry gesture of rebellion. The bow skidded, and the violin shrieked in pain. *(The piercing sound of an instrumental shriek; a note gone desperately awry.)* Like some torture victim refusing to comply.

THE FATHER. Our cat caught its tail in the screen door. Made the same sound.

THE PROFESSOR. Muti suggested we begin again. But our little prodigy refused. Eyes flashing behind his tiny horn-rims. So much fury locked inside that elfin body, it shook.

THE FATHER. Concert was canceled.

THE MOTHER. We took the first flight home.

THE FATHER. Kid didn't say a word.

THE MOTHER. Three hundred miles, not a peep.

THE FATHER. As soon as I opened the front door — whoosh, bang! — he ran upstairs, then a loud slam.

THE MOTHER. Hid away inside his room.

THE PROFESSOR. Like some martyr in self-imposed exile. To punish himself. To punish us.

THE FATHER. All because he'd missed a note. *(All four characters begin to speak in unison, their words hitting the air in a frenzy of noise. One by one, we pick out each "solo.")*

THE PROFESSOR. My reputation was wounded, to say the least. I wrote the Maestro a long letter of apology, expressing the fervent hope we could collaborate again. There would be other students, I lied. Perhaps Muti divined my desperation; perhaps it lifted off the stationery like some rancid perfume. Perhaps some dim-witted, slack-jawed secretary let it lie, orphaned, on his desk. Or a fateful error on my part; those infernal European postal codes. Whatever the reason ... I received no reply.

THE MOTHER. If I'd only known ... if I'd had any idea ... that was the last time I'd ever see my angel. If I would have taken a memory snapshot; just to freeze him for a moment in my mind.

Because — when I look at pictures of him now — he's not there. He's hovering just beyond them, like a ghost. I wiped his tears, I changed his diapers, I held those precious hands as he learned to take each tiny step. But now I can't feel him anymore. It's as though he were made of sand — just sand — and he keeps slipping through my fingers ...

THE DOCTOR. Without support from the private sector — in six, seven months — the Institute will be forced to close its doors. It's a personal loss, of course. But I've weathered disappointment before. What keeps me awake at night ... what tweaks at my conscience ... the collective loss. For a brief, unbelievable moment — a moment plucked from the pages of Clarke, of Asimov — we had the power to harness Fate. To breed our own destiny. The human genome was ours; it lay in our palm, winking, like some rarified jewel. One-of-a-kind. Countless-of-a-kind. For a moment, it was ours to control.

THE FATHER. His tuxedo's still hanging in the hall closet, next to mine. Some midget version of me, hanging in a black bag. His cummerbund was small; it could fit around my thigh. I was in the Petco; saw those gimmick suits for dogs. There was one — black velvet with a lace collar and studs running down the front — made me sick to my stomach, to tell you the truth. I was going to dry-clean his tux, to pack it away, but the wife wouldn't let me. She wants to keep it "as is"; like it's still got his residue ... his spirit ... in the fabric. *(Silence.)*

THE MOTHER. And then it began.

THE PROFESSOR. When I heard of the boy's demise, in some dark, corroded corner of my mind — I felt vindicated.

THE MOTHER. That night ... alone in his room ... high up at the top of the stairs ... he began to play. *(We hear the jaunty, insolent lilt of Paganini's* Rondo.*)*

THE MOTHER. *Rondo* this. *Rondo* that.

THE FATHER. Forwards. Backwards. At triple speed.

THE MOTHER. It rang through the house like some terrible alarm.

THE FATHER. He was hell-bent on proving something.

THE MOTHER. But to who?

THE FATHER. Paga-whosit was turning cartwheels in his grave.

THE MOTHER. His door was locked.

THE FATHER. Windows, too. Shades drawn.

THE MOTHER. By evening, the neighbors complained.

THE FATHER. What was I s'posed to do? Tear down a wall?

THE MOTHER. We felt foolish.

THE FATHER. Call out the fire department?

THE MOTHER. I was standing on the dining room table, pounding the ceiling with my shoe.

THE FATHER. Same damn piece, over and over and over and over and over …

THE MOTHER. We started slipping sheet music under the door hoping he'd play something — *anything* — new.

THE FATHER. Even tried bluegrass.

THE MOTHER. I refused to cook for him. "When he's weak from hunger," I said, "he'll have to come down."

THE FATHER. Kid wouldn't budge. *(A pause; The Mother and Father let the music wash over them.)*

THE MOTHER. We got used to it. That's the terrible truth.

THE FATHER. I'd be out, driving. I'd miss it.

THE MOTHER. It underscored our lives. Lunatic, I know. It became as natural to us as the sound of our own breathing. Then — when was it?

THE FATHER. Four A.M. in the middle of the third week.

THE MOTHER. He stopped playing. *Silence. (The music stops abruptly.)*

THE FATHER. It woke us up.

THE MOTHER. "Honey."

THE FATHER. "You go."

THE MOTHER. "We'll go together."

THE FATHER. I took a flashlight.

THE MOTHER. The stairs were so tall. The climb lasted hours.

THE FATHER. Door was ajar. In we went.

THE MOTHER. The flashlight rose and fell over the furniture. His trundle bed. His little red rocker. His music stand. No sign of him. Anywhere.

THE FATHER. Then we saw it.

THE MOTHER. It was lying in the center of the room.

THE FATHER. On the rug.

THE DOCTOR. Some days later, the parents brought it to me. Our lab performed a battery of tests.

THE PROFESSOR. I had to play it. *(The wildly distorted strains of Paganini's* Rondo. *Eerie and discordant.)* What remarkable sound! Haunting tones more reminiscent of castrati than your conventional fiddle.

THE DOCTOR. Its cellular composition matched that of the child.

THE PROFESSOR. But its appearance … grotesque.

THE DOCTOR. Atom for atom. It matched the child.

THE FATHER. There … on the rug … the thing was …

THE MOTHER. Tell them.

THE FATHER. It was still warm. *(The Auctioneer crosses to the coffin and opens it. A hot white light pours forth from it, like the parched sheen of highly polished bone. In its lid, the velvet indentations of a violin. The Auctioneer returns to his podium. The Professor approaches the casket. Gingerly, he looks inside. He describes what he sees.)*

THE PROFESSOR. Hollow bone. The neck and scroll twist like a femur. The pegs resemble finger joints, and the ribs of the instrument are unnervingly authentic. The string, stretched taut across its pale white body, has the unmistakable consistency of human hair. The tuners are tiny molars laid out in a grin. But the bow. The bow is truly shocking. It has an almost spinal curve; the backbone of a child. *(The Doctor and The Father step forward to meet The Professor. Finally — with great hesitancy — The Mother joins them. Solemnly, they all gaze into the coffin. The light illuminates them from beneath, casting an eerie glow across their faces.)*

THE FATHER. We shoulda known then.

THE PROFESSOR. Perhaps that's all he ever was. An instrument.

THE FATHER. Way back. We shoulda known.

THE PROFESSOR. Are we to blame? For anthropomorphosizing?

THE MOTHER. We never found him.

THE PROFESSOR. The violin is real. Did we imagine the child?

THE MOTHER. We never found our little boy. *(Slowly, The Mother, The Father, The Doctor and The Professor return to their music stands. The lights on them fade. Lights intensify on The Auctioneer, and on the bone violin. The auctioneer pounds his gavel a third time.)*

THE AUCTIONEER. We'll start the bidding at ten thousand … *(Blackout.)*

End of Play

UNWRAP YOUR CANDY
Part Two

UNWRAP YOUR CANDY
Part Two

In the darkness, a beat following "Lot 13: The Bone Violin."
Suddenly, a pin spot illuminates an actual, unsuspecting
audience member seated in the house. We hear his or her
thoughts, telegraphed loudly over the theater's sound system:

THE WOULD-BE GROCERY SHOPPER. Milk. Orange juice.
Sour cream, for that dip you like so much. Corn flakes. Two dou-
ble-A batteries. Cat food. Deodorant. Häagen-Dazs. Uh, no, better not. Grapefruit. Antibacterial soap. Moist towelettes, just to
have, just to carry. Campbell's mushroom soup, for that casserole.
Some celery root and some cilantro ... *(The pin spots goes out, only
to reappear on yet another member of the audience.)*
THE WISHFUL THINKER. I could've been an actor. All those
elocution lessons. And I've always had exceptional posture. Those
poetry readings I used to give on my birthday ... Actors have such
glamorous lives. So bohemian. So wild. I bet this entire cast is
sleeping together. My God, the things we don't know. That we're
not privy to, sitting out here in the dark. I bet — backstage — it's
an orgy, every night. *(Once again, the light goes out only to ignite
upon someone else:)*
THE RELUCTANT PARTICIPANT. Audience participation?
No one told me this had audience participation. I wouldn't
have come. This isn't the *Blue Man Group*. This isn't *Fool
Moon*. If I'd wanted to act, I'd be up there on the stage. Turn
that light *off*. Turn it off. *Now. Don't look at me.* Everybody,
stop looking. *Off. Off. I want it off ... Okay, we get the gag,
everybody gets the gag ...* I'm being a good sport. Ha-ha. Funny,
funny. *NOW TURN THAT DAMN LIGHT OFF ... (And the*

light goes out, quickly, as the next play in the evening's line-up —
"Wildwood Park" — commences.)

End of Part Two

WILDWOOD PARK

"Repulsion is the sentry that
guards the gate to all that we
most desire."

—*Salvador Dalí*

CHARACTERS

MS. HAVILAND — A realtor. She is middle-aged, a working mother. She wears an attractive, quilted jacket, a navy skirt and cloissonné jewelry. Her shoes are sensible, for walking.

DR. SIMIAN — A prospective buyer. He is of indeterminate age and wears an expensive suit. He is disarmingly handsome.

TIME

Now.

PLACE

The stage is bare. The architecture, the furnishings and the props of the play are all invisible, and indicated by the actors through gesture — not in an overly-demonstrative or "mime" fashion, but simply and clearly, with minimal movement. Even when specific mention is made in the text of nightstands, vanities or fireplaces, these things are not seen; they are created through inference and the power of suggestion.

WILDWOOD PARK

A stark, sunny day. In the distance, the sound of suburban children at play. Both Ms. Haviland and Dr. Simian wear dark glasses to shield their eyes from the offending light. They stand side by side, in front of the "house," gazing up at its exterior.

DR. SIMIAN. The neighborhood. It exceeds my expectations. The trees are symmetrical. The mail-boxes have tiny flags. Along the alley, the trash cans all have matching lids.

MS. HAVILAND. It's well-tended.

DR. SIMIAN. It's *almost* perfection, isn't it? *(Dr. Simian smiles at Ms. Haviland. She does not return the gesture. There is a stiff pause.)*

MS. HAVILAND. How did you hear about this listing?

DR. SIMIAN. The newspaper.

MS. HAVILAND. The *real-estate* section?

DR. SIMIAN. Yes.

MS. HAVILAND. That's not possible. Boulevard Realty ... in the interest of discretion ... in the interest of *taste* ... opted not to publish this particular address. So when you called, when you called with your *specific* request ...

DR. SIMIAN. The ... ah ... front page, Ms. Haviland. That is how I knew. I realized ... I *surmised* ... the house would be for sale.

MS. HAVILAND. Did you?

DR. SIMIAN. And your firm ... your size, your reputation ... what other firm, I asked myself ...

MS. HAVILAND. Well. What other firm *in this area* ...

DR. SIMIAN. Surely I am not alone. You must admit, public pre-occupation with ... *this house* ... I am not the first prospective buyer whose interest was initially piqued by reports of an alto-gether different nature ...

31

MS. HAVILAND. No. You're not. *You most certainly are not. (A tense pause.)* Where have you been living?

DR. SIMIAN. Glen Ridge.

MS. HAVILAND. I'm not familiar with Glen Ridge.

DR. SIMIAN. No?

MS. HAVILAND. I have never even *heard* of Glen Ridge.

DR. SIMIAN. Beyond Ridge Falls. Near Beacon Ridge. Before Ridge Dale.

MS. HAVILAND. Suddenly you've decided to move?

DR. SIMIAN. Yes.

MS. HAVILAND. More room? Better schools? A sound investment strategy?

DR. SIMIAN. It's *time.*

MS. HAVILAND. Why *now?*

DR. SIMIAN. I've weathered a change in status.

MS. HAVILAND. Marital? Professional?

DR. SIMIAN. Both.

MS. HAVILAND. I hope it works out. For the best.

DR. SIMIAN. I hope. *(Another stilted pause.)*

MS. HAVILAND. I'd like to point out some of the exterior features of the house, if I may. It's a Colonial, of course. The portico dates back to the Revolutionary War. Wildwood Park's own *Monticello.* Of course, the drainage system, the storm windows, the pool, the carport — that's all contemporary.

DR. SIMIAN. Conservative, isn't it?

MS. HAVILAND. Classic. Beyond faddish. A constant. *(Ms. Haviland points.)* Notice the weathercock.

DR. SIMIAN. Where? I don't see ... I can't quite ...

MS. HAVILAND. The rooster.

DR. SIMIAN. The glare ...

MS. HAVILAND. The *silhouette.*

DR. SIMIAN. The sun's so *white* ...

MS. HAVILAND. Left of the chimney. *(Dr. Simian uses his hands like a visor, shielding his eyes. He spots the weather vane.)*

DR. SIMIAN. Ah! Yes!

MS. HAVILAND. It wasn't bought; it was commissioned.

DR. SIMIAN. Impressive.

MS. HAVILAND. This house belongs on the dollar bill. *(Another pause.)* What sort of work do you do?

DR. SIMIAN. Medical.

MS. HAVILAND. You're not a journalist?

DR. SIMIAN. Should I be? *(Ms. Haviland glances from left to right. She speaks in a low, confidential tone.)*

MS. HAVILAND. I have to ask ...

DR. SIMIAN. Yes?

MS. HAVILAND. You're not *undercover*, are you?

DR. SIMIAN. Under what?

MS. HAVILAND. You're not *wearing a wire?*

DR. SIMIAN. Excuse me?

MS. HAVILAND. You are not an *opportunist,* are you?

DR. SIMIAN. I rather expected I'd be asking the questions this afternoon.

MS. HAVILAND. I've learned the hard way, Dr. Simian. I can't be too careful. A few weeks ago, a man came, requesting to see the house. He brought a camcorder. He told me that his wife was back home, in Terra Haute, and that he intended to mail the tape back to her, before deciding. Well. You can imagine my surprise, when a few days later, I turned on the television, one of those alarmist news programs, and there it was. Edited. With an ominous soundtrack.

DR. SIMIAN. He'd sold the tape?

MS. HAVILAND. So forgive me if I exert caution.

DR. SIMIAN. My sole interest, Ms. Haviland, is in purchasing a home.

MS. HAVILAND. Thank goodness.

DR. SIMIAN. I am far more invested in a firm foundation, a basement which does not leak, a patio for summer parties than I am in ... *the unsavory.*

MS. HAVILAND. Count yourself among a rarefied few.

DR. SIMIAN. If you distrust my *sincerity* ...

MS. HAVILAND. I didn't say that.

DR. SIMIAN. I am *eager* to relocate. I have an *approved loan.* My intentions could not be more *serious.*

MS. HAVILAND. I am *relieved.*

DR. SIMIAN. Would you care to see my correspondence with the bank? A copy of my current mortgage?

MS. HAVILAND. Please. I —

DR. SIMIAN. Proof positive. The listing for my own home in *The Town Tattler.*

MS. HAVILAND. That isn't necessary. *(Dr. Simian pulls a folded newspaper from his inner breast pocket.)*

DR. SIMIAN. *(Reading:)* "Glen Ridge Charmer: Raised ranch, designed with family in mind. Three bedroom, two and half bath, breakfast nook with skylight, basement rec room — "

MS. HAVILAND. I *apologize. (Dr. Simian slaps the paper against his hand twice, to flatten it. He re-folds it, and returns it to his pocket. Another short pause.)*

DR. SIMIAN. I would be less than honest —

MS. HAVILAND. *(Quickly:)* Yes?

DR. SIMIAN. — if I didn't confess to an ulterior motive.

MS. HAVILAND. I suspected as much.

DR. SIMIAN. The reason I chose this house … this *particular* house … with its rather … *notorious* … history …

MS. HAVILAND. Mm-hm?

DR. SIMIAN. I am … I am … I am a *bargain hunter.*

MS. HAVILAND. Oh. Well.

DR. SIMIAN. Correct me if I'm wrong, but I would assume, by-in-large, your average buyer would have, well … *trepidation.* A fear that the house had somehow been … *besmirched.* That it had absorbed its own history, and that it had somehow become … *a hard sell.* But I am not a superstitious person. Karma, aura. These things mean nothing to me.

MS. HAVILAND. *(With significance:)* I have an unhappy surprise for you, Doctor. *(Ms. Haviland makes a thumbs-up gesture, which suggests that the asking price has soared.)*

DR. SIMIAN. No.

MS. HAVILAND. *(Nodding:)* Oh yes.

DR. SIMIAN. That's shocking.

MS. HAVILAND. Through the roof.

DR. SIMIAN. Is that the culture? The culture-at-large? Is that what we've become?

MS. HAVILAND. *(As a vulture:)* Caaw! Caaw!

DR. SIMIAN. You'll make me a cynical man, Ms. Haviland.

MS. HAVILAND. 1120 Sycamore Avenue has made me a cynical woman.

DR. SIMIAN. And the property values. In the neighborhood. They are —

MS. HAVILAND. Holding their own.

DR. SIMIAN. My, my.

MS. HAVILAND. Wildwood Park has not changed. It is the same enclave it always was. The traffic, of course, is heavier.

DR. SIMIAN. People ignore the blockades.

MS. HAVILAND. It's a constant battle.

DR. SIMIAN. License plates from Iowa. From California.

MS. HAVILAND. The furor will die down. By the time you're ready to take occupancy … should you decide to pursue the house … the traffic will taper, I assure you …

DR. SIMIAN. Naturally.

MS. HAVILAND. We still boast excellent schools. And I don't have to tell you, Doctor, the shopping in our little town is world-class. We have our own library. Our own post office. Our own women's auxiliary, and our own police force.

DR. SIMIAN. I couldn't help noticing. At the curb. The squad car.

MS. HAVILAND. A precaution against vandalism. A few weeks ago — a rock, some spray paint. *Eggs.*

DR. SIMIAN. I see.

MS. HAVILAND. An isolated incident.

DR. SIMIAN. It's to be expected.

MS. HAVILAND. It gives me great civic pride, Dr. Simian, to tell you that — for weeks — the front porch was teeming with candles. Bouquets. My own daughter made a wreath from sapling twigs. I was moved. *(A pause.)* Shall we go inside?

DR. SIMIAN. Please. *(Ms. Haviland begins the complicated process of opening the door.)*

MS. HAVILAND. You'll notice there are two double-bolts, with pick-proof cylinders. In addition, the house has a twenty-four-hour, fully computerized security system with built-in alarm, automatic police and fire notification, and an electronic fence.

DR. SIMIAN. These precautions. They are … recent?

MS. HAVILAND. Yes. They are *new.* They were not here *before.* *(Another brief pause.)* Shall we? *(They "enter" the house. As Ms. Haviland and Dr. Simian move from room to room throughout the house, it's as though they are tokens on a board game, moving through*

35

implied three-dimensional space.) Eight thousand square feet, Doctor. Five bedrooms, four and a half baths. *(Ms. Haviland makes an extravagant gesture, indicating the vast expanse of the front hall.)* Notice the upward sweep of the foyer. The walls rise the full height of the house. The candelabra; that's brass. And look at the sunlight streaming down. We're flooded, aren't we? We're drowning in light. *(Ms. Haviland removes her sunglasses.)* Dr. Simian. Your glasses. The color scheme.

DR. SIMIAN. Safe now, isn't it? *(Dr. Simian removes his glasses and slips them into his breast pocket.)* And that?

MS. HAVILAND. Where?

DR. SIMIAN. Above the arch.

MS. HAVILAND. Ah, yes. *That.* It's Pennsylvania Dutch. A touch of *whimsy.*

DR. SIMIAN. What is it?

MS. HAVILAND. *Oh, dear.*

DR. SIMIAN. You're blushing.

MS. HAVILAND. It's a hex sign. *That is a hex sign.*

DR. SIMIAN. No.

MS. HAVILAND. For *good* luck.

DR. SIMIAN. One can't help thinking —

MS. HAVILAND. Please. Don't. *(Dr. Simian wanders ahead.)*

DR. SIMIAN. Is this the living room?

MS. HAVILAND. I must ask you, *don't barrel through.*

DR. SIMIAN. Forgive me.

MS. HAVILAND. I am conducting the tour.

DR. SIMIAN. Of course.

MS. HAVILAND. "Follow the Leader." *Indulge me.* Watch your step.

DR. SIMIAN. Thank you. *(They "enter" the living room.)*

MS. HAVILAND. An exquisite space, Doctor. Floor-length windows. On the ceiling, rosettes. And the fireplace. You'll note its size. Its grandeur. Quarried marble. Venetian, I think. *(Dr. Simian runs his hand along the mantelpiece.)*

DR. SIMIAN. A substantial mantel.

MS. HAVILAND. Yes.

DR. SIMIAN. Can it support sculpture? Can it support *object d' art?*

MS. HAVILAND. *(Curtly.)* I think you can *gauge,* Doctor.

DR. SIMIAN. The house is still furnished.

MS. HAVILAND. Not for long.

DR. SIMIAN. It looks … *inhabited.*

MS. HAVILAND. Things happened so quickly. The house was placed on the market so soon.

DR. SIMIAN. This room reminds me, Ms. Haviland, of an exhibit in a museum. The stillness. Its past hanging heavy in the air, unspoken.

MS. HAVILAND. There was of course, a will, provisions were naturally made, but in the absence of any … *beneficiaries* … the furniture will be sold at auction.

DR. SIMIAN. Aha.

MS. HAVILAND. The proceeds will benefit the Children's Legal Defense Fund.

DR. SIMIAN. An appropriate gesture.

MS. HAVILAND. If … *when* it is recovered … after its release from evidence … the Nubian statuette is expected to fetch a startling sum.

DR. SIMIAN. Surprise, surprise.

MS. HAVILAND. "Who," I ask myself. "Who would buy — "

DR. SIMIAN. Our society is predatory.

MS. HAVILAND. I'd almost bid on it myself. So I could take it home. So I could take it home with me, and with my husband's hammer —

DR. SIMIAN. *Yes.*

MS. HAVILAND. I'd pay a hefty sum, just for the pleasure of see-ing it *destroyed.*

DR. SIMIAN. Do you know, Ms. Haviland, the totems of our time?

MS. HAVILAND. The "totems"?

DR. SIMIAN. In Milwaukee, a stock pot on the stove. In Brentwood, an errant glove.

MS. HAVILAND. And among them …

DR. SIMIAN. … yes …

MS. HAVILAND. … in Wildwood Park …

DR. SIMIAN. … exactly …

MS. HAVILAND. A Nubian statuette. *(They "enter" the dining room.)* You'll notice how the living room segues into the dining room. Dignified, isn't it? *Vintage.* You can comfortably seat up to twenty-four. Those sconces are from a tavern in the Hudson River Valley, circa 1890. You'd never guess ... *(Ms. Haviland toys with a light switch.)* ... they're on a dimmer.

DR. SIMIAN. The kitchen can't be far behind.

MS. HAVILAND. Careful; that door swings. *(They "enter" the kitchen.)* A rustic look, but with every modern convenience. An electric oven, an industrial range, a microwave, and — for "old world" effect, a touch of antique romance — a wood-burning stove. Charming, yes? The cabinets are cherry wood, and the countertops are Mexican tile. And you'll note, there's an island ... cherry, too, with a granite top, pull-out shelves below, and of course ... a ... you see it, there ... with a ... a ... *oh, dear ...*

DR. SIMIAN. A what?

MS. HAVILAND. A *block.*

DR. SIMIAN. A block?

MS. HAVILAND. A *butcher* block. *(Ms. Haviland smiles a guilty smile.)*

DR. SIMIAN. Why, Ms. Haviland.

MS. HAVILAND. I'm horrible.

DR. SIMIAN. You've made a pun.

MS. HAVILAND. I'm a monster.

DR. SIMIAN. A pun, that's all.

MS. HAVILAND. I should have my tongue *cut out.* *(Ms. Haviland suppresses a giggle.)* Oh, there. I've done it again.

DR. SIMIAN. You're *giddy.*

MS. HAVILAND. Shame on me. Shame on us both.

DR. SIMIAN. Humor, Ms. Haviland, fortifies. *(Ms. Haviland wipes tears from her eyes, composing herself.)*

MS. HAVILAND. This house, all day, every day. Dodging past the news vans. Those rapacious tourists. I fight my way past. *I have business here.* If it's made me loopy, Doctor, then I have every right to be.

DR. SIMIAN. Bravo.

MS. HAVILAND. My husband says it's nerves. My husband says all those infernal shutterbugs, all those flashbulbs, they've *seared* my *brain.*

DR. SIMIAN. A fanciful thought, Ms. Haviland.

MS. HAVILAND. My husband tells me that I take things to

heart. That I should go on *automatic.* That is easy, Doctor, for *my* husband to *say.* It is, after all, his *forte. (Ms. Haviland snorts a laugh, a little bark, which afterwards makes her cheeks burn red.)*

DR. SIMIAN. I'd like to see the master bedroom.

MS. HAVILAND. *(Sadly.)* I'm exhausted. Frayed. That's the *truth.*

DR. SIMIAN. The bedroom, please.

MS. HAVILAND. But you haven't seen the den. You haven't seen the home office, the playroom, the maid's suite — *(Dr. Simian leaves the kitchen. Ms. Haviland follows, suddenly strident.) Don't charge ahead!*

DR. SIMIAN. I'm overeager.

MS. HAVILAND. I can't have people *wander.* I can't have people *traipsing through.*

DR. SIMIAN. I might go nosing in the linen cupboards.

MS. HAVILAND. Don't be absurd; it's not that.

DR. SIMIAN. I might empty the medicine chest.

MS. HAVILAND. *It's not that at all.*

DR. SIMIAN. I might pirate away knickknacks, and open a souvenir stand on the corner.

MS. HAVILAND. I am responsible for the house, and its contents. I have *police* on my back. There are *attorneys.* A *battalion* of *lawyers.* Under the circumstances, it is an *overwhelming* duty.

DR. SIMIAN. I was insensitive.

MS. HAVILAND. My psychiatrist is *worried.* She *fears* for my *safety.* I am on *tranquilizers.*

DR. SIMIAN. It must be a strain. *(They "enter" the master bedroom.)*

MS. HAVILAND. There are ceiling fans in all the bedrooms. You'll find that saves a fortune in cooling costs during the summer. A walk-in closet, which I daresay is larger than my living room.

DR. SIMIAN. Poignant, isn't it?

MS. HAVILAND. What?

DR. SIMIAN. There. On the floor, by the bed. *(Dr. Simian points:)* Empty shoes. *(A palpable chill descends in the room.)*

DR. SIMIAN. This is where it began, yes?

MS. HAVILAND. *(Alarmed:) I beg your pardon? (The following dialogue is rapid-fire, accelerating in speed, a crescendo.)*

DR. SIMIAN. The balcony doors.

MS. HAVILAND. I'd rather not.

DR. SIMIAN. They were left ajar? They were pried open?

MS. HAVILAND. You know I don't *approve* ... I don't *appreciate* ...

DR. SIMIAN. Around the lock, scuffs. Gouges.

MS. HAVILAND. I'm here to show the house. I'm not a *detective*. I am not a *talk show host*.

DR. SIMIAN. Forgive me. But I couldn't help noticing — there — on the wainscoting —

MS. HAVILAND. The paint has been retouched.

DR. SIMIAN. Along the molding —

MS. HAVILAND. The carpets have all been shampooed.

DR. SIMIAN. Traces exist.

MS. HAVILAND. No. Where?

DR. SIMIAN. *Splotches.*

MS. HAVILAND. *There is nothing to notice.*

DR. SIMIAN. There. On the edge. Rimming the baseboards ...

MS. HAVILAND. *I don't see a thing.*

DR. SIMIAN. The electrical outlets. Where are they?

MS. HAVILAND. *(Frightened:) What?*

DR. SIMIAN. It's a fair question.

MS. HAVILAND. It's a *taunt*. It's a *jibe*.

DR. SIMIAN. For *lamps*. For *clock-radios*. A *laptop*. These things require *voltage*.

MS. HAVILAND. All sorts of *appliances* require voltage, Dr. Simian. ALL SORTS.

DR. SIMIAN. A heating pad, perhaps! An electric blanket! Nothing menacing, nothing *pneumatic*.

MS. HAVILAND. Don't be *facetious*, Doctor.

DR. SIMIAN. SHOW ME.

MS. HAVILAND. *Please!*

DR. SIMIAN. *WHERE?*

MS. HAVILAND. Behind the headboard. And there. Under the vanity. *(A short rest. Dr. Simian goes to the vanity table. He gets down on his hands and knees and looks beneath it.)*

DR. SIMIAN. The wall plate. It's scorched.

MS. HAVILAND. What did you expect? It was *overburdened*, it was profoundly *misused*.

DR. SIMIAN. Hidden down here. Out of sight, out of mind?

MS. HAVILAND. There are still a few details …

DR. SIMIAN. A few *vestiges?*

MS. HAVILAND. A few REPAIRS. *(Dr. Simian stands up. He looks in the mirror of the vanity, back at Ms. Haviland's reflection.)*

DR. SIMIAN. She was a singer for a while, wasn't she? She was on television in New York.

MS. HAVILAND. Dr. Simian, if you have inquiries about the house, about its *architecture*, its *design,* its *upkeep* —

DR. SIMIAN. She sold thigh cream, and overcame personal problems. And he made a fortune in junk bonds.

MS. HAVILAND. I'm sure I don't know.

DR. SIMIAN. Of course you know. *Everybody knows.*

MS. HAVILAND. I'm not *interested.*

DR. SIMIAN. You can't flip on the radio, you can't watch the news —

MS. HAVILAND. I *mute,* Doctor.

DR. SIMIAN. Even pick up a paper —

MS. HAVILAND. Because of my *professional obligations* … my *necessary involvement* … there are certain things I'd rather *not* know … *(Dr. Simian notices something on the wall. He points:)*

DR. SIMIAN. The little one. The youngest. The girl.

MS. HAVILAND. I have recommended to my employer that we remove these photographs. They're unnerving. Prospective buyers are unhinged. *(Dr. Simian traces the shape of the frame on the wall with his finger.)*

DR. SIMIAN. Freckles. A gap tooth.

MS. HAVILAND. Their eyes follow you. No matter where you turn.

DR. SIMIAN. What was her name?

MS. HAVILAND. All day, every day, they stare me down. Here at work. In *this* room. Outside, too. In line at the grocery store, the tabloids. On *T-shirts,* for God's sake, they've even been *silk-screened* … *(Dr. Simian notices another picture, this one on the nightstand. He approaches it and picks it up.)*

DR. SIMIAN. Here she is again, in a pageant of some kind.

MS. HAVILAND. *Put that down!*

DR. SIMIAN. Look at her. She's dressed as a radish. She's singing.

MS. HAVILAND. *You're not supposed to touch things!*

DR. SIMIAN.   Oh, and look. Washing the family dog. *(Dr. Simian puts the picture back in its place.)* Is it true? *Even the dog?*

MS. HAVILAND.   *You are disturbing things ... me ...*

DR. SIMIAN.   The police posit that, sometime after three, she ... the girl ... heard a sound. If only she'd opted to hide under the bed, they said, if only she'd run out the back door, they said, if only her little legs — *(Ms. Haviland relents, and cuts him off.)*

MS. HAVILAND.   *Heather. (A pause.)* Her name was Heather.

DR. SIMIAN.   Take me to the nursery. *(Another pause.)*

MS. HAVILAND.   Do you have *children,* Dr. Simian?

DR. SIMIAN.   More questions, Ms. Haviland?

MS. HAVILAND.   Because if you don't have children ... if you don't have *young* children ... then the nursery is *irrelevant.*

DR. SIMIAN.   Surely you are not offering the house on a room-by-room basis.

MS. HAVILAND.   Don't insult me, Doctor.

DR. SIMIAN.   I am interested in the entire structure. Not a portion thereof.

MS. HAVILAND.   It's just, you've hardly inspected the house. The living room, the kitchen, the dining room, and nary a remark. "He's bound to have questions about the plumbing," I say to myself, "and radon, and chimney flues. He'll want to know about the new roof, about winter insulation." *But no!*

DR. SIMIAN.   Ms. Haviland, I —

MS. HAVILAND.   *Oh, no!* With you it's all ... hex signs ... and hollow shoes ... and *little girls.*

DR. SIMIAN.   There are still whole rooms —

MS. HAVILAND.   The tour is over.

DR. SIMIAN.   *Entire wings —*

MS. HAVILAND.   It's half-past-five.

DR. SIMIAN.   The backyard. The guest house.

MS. HAVILAND.   The workday has come to a close.

DR. SIMIAN.   I've driven a great distance —

MS. HAVILAND.   Please leave.

DR. SIMIAN.   I can't readily arrange a second visit —

MS. HAVILAND.   Wildwood Park is a private community. A discreet community. It is not some sordid *theme park,* Doctor. It is not a *freak show,* with its tent flaps spread — no, *torn* — open for the nation's *amusement*. It is not some *dime store, penny-dreadful, Stephen King* —

DR. SIMIAN. A daughter, six, and a son, eight. *(A pause. Ms. Haviland blushes. Slowly and definitively — like a lawyer giving a summation of evidence — Dr. Simian continues.)* My daughter's name is Sarah. She has a widow's peak, hazel eyes and what at first might seem like an extra appendage but which, upon closer examination, reveals itself to be a very old, very odorous stuffed bear, a veteran of her bouts with the flu, the washing machine and even a long, torturous night spent, abandoned, in the supermarket. He has one eye, and leaves an unmistakable trail of fleece wherever he goes. His name, should you require it for the record, is Mister Pete. My son is Joshua. Because he was slow to walk, he was misdiagnosed with cerebral palsy, and it gave us quite a scare. Now he is graceful and long of limb. He is obsessed with choo-choo trains. The court — at the recommendation of my wife's psychologist — has granted custody solely to me. *(A long pause. Ms. Haviland swallows, hard. Her face is pinched. Finally:)*

MS. HAVILAND. It's upstairs. *(They climb in silence up an invisible flight of stairs to the nursery. Finally, they enter. The sound of children playing in the street wafts through an open window.)* The wallpaper is a pale green candy-stripe, suitable for a boy or girl. The border is Beatrix Potter. Window guards, of course. An intercom, so wherever you are in the house, you never feel far away. The children have their own bath. The basin is low, and the tub has a rail. As you can see, the emphasis here ... the design insures ... *attempts* to insure ... a child's *safety. (Ms. Haviland sighs, heavily.)* I want *desperately* to sell this house. I like fretting over parquet, and measuring square feet, and judging closet space. I do not like being a *sentinel.* I do not like standing by, quietly as people *gape* and *mock* and *jeer.* It's a disease, Doctor, and it is contagious, and some days, it's true, I fear *I am catching it.* This is not a *movie.* This is not *television. (Ms. Haviland cries, softly.)* What I do is necessary. Houses are bought and sold. But sometimes ... because it is so recent ... because it is so far *beyond* tragedy ... what I do here feels like *desecration.* Walking in their tracks. Sifting through their things. *Oh, God, forgive me.*

DR. SIMIAN. Did you know the victims, Ms. Haviland?

MS. HAVILAND. No.

DR. SIMIAN. Even a passing acquaintance?

MS. HAVILAND. No.

DR. SIMIAN. Then permit me to suggest ... this unfortunate event wields far greater power over you than perhaps it should.

MS. HAVILAND. *It's all I think about.* I have my own husband, my own children, we're remodeling our place on the Eastern shore, my mother has *cancer* — these things, they are *the substance of my life* — and now they are merely *distractions* to keep me from *obsessing ... Why that night? Why those children? The parents, were they spared the sight, were they taken first, or were they forced to witness ... And ... this, Doctor, haunts me the most ... what sort of man ... what kind of brute creature ...*

DR. SIMIAN. Anyone, I suppose, would wonder.

MS. HAVILAND. It's worse than *wondering.* Far more *extreme. (Ms. Haviland cannot continue. She musters strength, and then:)* Once ... a canceled appointment ... I barricaded the front door ... reset the alarm ... drew the blinds ... from her closet, a robe, blue with pink piping ... and I sat in the study ... swathed in her smell ... poring through family albums. Birthdays. Christmases. The first day at school, afternoons at the fair, anniversary notes, private, still perfumed ... They were not mine, but they *could've* been mine, they *might as well have been* mine ... I am such a *hypocrite,* Doctor.

DR. SIMIAN. *(Soothing.)* It's all right.

MS. HAVILAND. I sat, alone in this house, with the lights out, and I waited.

DR. SIMIAN. For what?

MS. HAVILAND. The balcony door to open. The soft, almost noiseless crunch of rubber soles on white shag ...

DR. SIMIAN. Why?

MS. HAVILAND. *If God gave me the chance to see evil, Doctor, then I would look. And that's a terrible thing to know about oneself. (Ms. Haviland looks at Dr. Simian pleadingly. He responds in a tender voice.)*

DR. SIMIAN. You are ...

MS. HAVILAND. Go ahead. Say it.

DR. SIMIAN. *(Enigmatic now.)* You are a *very bad* little monkey.

MS. HAVILAND. I want my own life *back*. My own *concerns*. *(Dr. Simian takes her hand. Ms. Haviland takes a moment to calm herself.)*

DR. SIMIAN. Take a breath. We don't have to move.

MS. HAVILAND. A new family. Here. That would be nice. An *antidote*, yes, Doctor? Isn't that the word? I hope that you will contemplate this house. I hope that with all my heart.

DR. SIMIAN. I intend to.

MS. HAVILAND. I would like … I would like to be free of this. And I would like you …

DR. SIMIAN. Yes?

MS. HAVILAND. You … and your children … a fresh start.

DR. SIMIAN. Remember, Ms. Haviland that you have your *own* home. Your own *retreat*.

MS. HAVILAND. *(Consoled.)* Yes. *(Dr. Simian slips his dark glasses out of his pocket. He puts them back on.)*

DR. SIMIAN. Would you see me to the porch?

MS. HAVILAND. My pleasure, Doctor. *(Again, they backtrack in silence, this time without any obvious tension. They leave the house and step outside onto the porch.)* I'm embarrassed. My employer.

DR. SIMIAN. The robe, the snapshots.

MS. HAVILAND. If they knew …

DR. SIMIAN. Not a word.

MS. HAVILAND. Here's my card. If you have any question, don't hesitate.

DR. SIMIAN. *(Taking the card.)* I won't.

MS. HAVILAND. I'm sorry. My *display*.

DR. SIMIAN. Don't mention it.

MS. HAVILAND. I've shown you quite an afternoon, haven't I?

DR. SIMIAN. Quite.

MS. HAVILAND. You. A *stranger*.

DR. SIMIAN. I did wonder —

MS. HAVILAND. Yes?

DR. SIMIAN. A musing. A curiosity. Nothing pragmatic. Nothing "nuts and bolts."

MS. HAVILAND. Please.

DR. SIMIAN. One thing concerns me.

MS. HAVILAND. Oh?

DR. SIMIAN. No arrest. No conviction.

MS. HAVILAND. Sadly enough.

DR. SIMIAN. No substantive leads.

MS. HAVILAND. Every day, we pray.

DR. SIMIAN. As you suggest ... there exists the possibility of ... well, the perpetrator ... he might return.

MS. HAVILAND. I see my paranoia has spread.

DR. SIMIAN. No, no. Your *prescience*. It's often been documented. Many a criminal — in spite of the immense risk — will return to the scene of the crime.

MS. HAVILAND. I can't *imagine* ...

DR. SIMIAN. Regardless of the alarms. The reversible bolts. The electronic fences. Even the squad car at the curb.

MS. HAVILAND. But *why?*

DR. SIMIAN. All in pursuit of the covert thrill that comes with the successful commission of a wrongful act.

MS. HAVILAND. Is that *true?* Is that what they *say?*

DR. SIMIAN. It would not shock me to learn, Ms. Haviland, that you yourself had escorted the culprit through these halls.

MS. HAVILAND. It is a good thing that I am so *thorough*, Doctor. So *vigilant.*

DR. SIMIAN. He feigns interest in the housing market. Comes well-armed, perhaps, with the *classifieds.* You interrogate him, and for every question, he has a ready quip. He is from an obscure town. He is a banker. No. A lawyer. No. *A doctor. (Ms. Haviland freezes. Her whole body seems to clench. Dr. Simian takes a step closer to her.)*

MS. HAVILAND. *Yes. (Dr. Simian takes another step, even closer.)*

DR. SIMIAN. He is newly married. No. Expecting a baby.

MS. HAVILAND. No. *Separated. (And another step closer.)*

DR. SIMIAN. He has grown daughters. No. Adopted sons. No — *(Dr. Simian is so near, she can feel his breath.)*

MS. HAVILAND. *A boy and a girl. One of each. Her name, it begins with an "S" ... she has a toy, an old ... a very beloved ... it's plush ... Mister Somebody ... (Dr. Simian cocks an eyebrow and waits for Ms. Haviland to finish.) I can't ... I don't ... oh, God ... (Dr. Simian reaches down and takes her hand. He separates her fingers with his own, and intertwines them. He speaks in a sensuous, hypnotic tone.*

46

Deep within Ms. Haviland, continental plates begin to shift.)

DR. SIMIAN. You usher him over the threshold. As you patter on — stucco and mini-blinds and Formica and chintz — with each step he's reliving, with a kind of salacious glee, the very night he thwarted every fragile notion of civilized behavior. The very night he let loose the constraints of his own base nature, and made the very darkest kind of history. *(With his free hand, gently, Dr. Simian takes Ms. Haviland by the chin. He raises her face to meet his. They stare at one another.)* Tell me. *Do you ever consider that possibility?*

MS. HAVILAND. No. I do not.

DR. SIMIAN. Perhaps you should.

MS. HAVILAND. *I emphatically do not.* I can't … *afford* … to entertain such … *notions.* It would render my job untenable.

DR. SIMIAN. Yes.

MS. HAVILAND. It would induce paralysis. It would hold me captive.

DR. SIMIAN. Precisely.

MS. HAVILAND. *I cannot live my life that way.*

DR. SIMIAN. You're a wise woman. *(Ms. Haviland speaks with a very slight, almost imperceptible tremor.)*

MS. HAVILAND. I hope that you will consider this house. I hope that you are in the market, and I hope that you will buy. *(Dr. Simian nods in the direction of the squad car.)*

DR. SIMIAN. Perhaps, when I leave, you'll offer the policeman a cup of coffee.

MS. HAVILAND. No.

DR. SIMIAN. Perhaps you'll have a conversation.

MS. HAVILAND. We've never met. I see him every morning, but we've never met.

DR. SIMIAN. Perhaps today is the day.

MS. HAVILAND. I do not know him.

DR. SIMIAN. That doesn't preclude a polite introduction.

MS. HAVILAND. I know *you*, Doctor.

DR. SIMIAN. Thank you.

MS. HAVILAND. You are the man whom I know.

DR. SIMIAN. Thank you *so much*. *(Dr. Simian lets her hand go. He takes a step back. Ms. Haviland wavers, starts to melt into him. She holds herself back.)* It's been a lovely afternoon. And the house.

47

The house is beautiful. *(Dr. Simian turns to leave. Ms. Haviland calls him back.)*

MS. HAVILAND. You're interested, then?

DR. SIMIAN. Yes. *(Again, Dr. Simian turns to go. Again, Ms. Haviland stops him.)*

MS. HAVILAND. *(Impulsively.)* Dr. Simian?

DR. SIMIAN. Ms. Haviland?

MS. HAVILAND. *(Darkly; almost seductively.)* You *are* interested? *(Dr. Simian smiles an enigmatic smile. He holds up Ms. Haviland's business card. With deliberate slowness, he slips it into his breast pocket. He pats his heart three times. They stare at one another a long time. Finally, Dr. Simian leaves. Ms. Haviland lingers after him for a moment. Slowly, she turns back to gaze at the house. Slow fade to black.)*

End of Play

UNWRAP YOUR CANDY
Part Three

UNWRAP YOUR CANDY
Part Three

In the darkness, a beat following "Wildwood Park." Suddenly, another pin spot beams down on a theater-goer:

THE TRADITIONALIST. Call me old-fashioned, but I like plays with a beginning, a middle and an end. With characters you'd be proud to have in your home. Something upbeat, something to live for. You know what I just loved? *The Music Man.* *(Singing softly.)* Seventy-six trombones lead the big parade ... while a hundred and ten coronets played along ... *(And again:)*
THE DIE-HARD FAN. I'm in love with that actress. From the last play. I've seen every play she's ever done, from basements in the East Village all the way to Broadway. The theater wouldn't give me her home number, not over the telephone, but what do you know — *she's actually listed!* She doesn't know I'm here tonight. I'm going to surprise her. I left her a little kitten from the Humane Society with a big pink bow, in a basket. The stage manager promised to give it to her. I hope she likes cats. I'll be waiting outside after, by the curb. *(Once again, the light goes out. This time — when it comes on again — it shines upon an empty theater seat in the rear of the house.)*
THE WALK-OUT. I just walked out. That's right. I'm not here! This seat's empty! Warm, but empty! Got up and left while the getting was good. The restaurants are all still half-empty, at least for another hour. Plenty of cabs. I'm in one now! Hey, buddy, honk the horn! *(Indiscernible exchange with an unwilling cabbie:)* No, go ahead, do it. *(Sound of a car horn honking.)* I'll be back home in bed by ten. And look at you all. *Suckers.* Stuck there, waiting. Me, I'm free — free — free!

End of Part Three

BABY TALK
A Case Study in One Act

CHARACTERS

THE PSYCHIATRIST — Compassionate, but alarmed at the content of this particular case.

THE HUSBAND — Befuddled. Where did it all go so terribly wrong?

ALICE — Attractive, surburban and eager to set the record straight.

THE BABY — An actor with a cigarette, a lighter and a glass of Scotch.

SETTING

Two stools, one for mother and one for baby. A microphone.

BABY TALK
A Case Study in One Act

A psychiatrist in a white lab coat and hospital name-tag stands in a pool of light.

THE PSYCHIATRIST. I'd like to bring your attention to Case Number 696724-B. *(He surveys the audience to ensure everyone has located the proper case file.)* A woman — approximately twenty-two years old, one hundred and five pounds, five feet, five inches tall. No previous history of mental disturbance. Admitted by her husband on three separate occasions. Each time, he recounted a variety of behaviors associated with schizophrenia: auditory hallucinations, social affective disorder and avolition. His words weren't clinical — those are my own — but they were trenchant: *(The Husband steps forward into a light of his own. He's an affable fellow, pleasantly rumpled, with horn-rims and a ribbed cotton sweater.)*
THE HUSBAND. My wife, she … ah … she has a funny habit of answering back to questions that nobody's asked.
THE PSYCHIATRIST. We'll call the subject "Alice." *(Lights rise on Alice, who sits on a low stool, her legs daintily crossed at the ankles. She knits. Alice is a pleasant-looking woman with shoulder-length hair, neatly combed and held in place by a striped headband. She smiles benignly.)* Alice became symptomatic at the time of her first — and only — pregnancy.
THE HUSBAND. One of her doctors — *(He turns to the Pyschiatrist, and says in a heartfelt tone:)* — not you, one of your colleagues, I've no complaints with you, none — *(The Psychiatrist nods in assent.)* — but one of her doctors said that she didn't want the baby. Well, that's simply not true. That's a gross distortion. She

wanted the baby more than anything. We had a big calendar up in the kitchen, and the big yellow boxes, rimmed with Highlighter: those were —

ALICE. — ovulation days!

THE HUSBAND. *(Grinning.)* Those days, I even came home on my lunch hour. I felt like a machine; like a pneumatic piston. *(The Husband cranks his arm and makes the sound of a machine.)* I liked feeling that way.

ALICE. I was a puzzle and somehow I knew that it — my baby — it would be the missing piece.

THE HUSBAND. One day — finally — the stick turned blue. Sky blue. I remember; she ran into the living room in nothing but an old pair of my pajama tops, holding the test aloft, like it was some kind of victory banner

ALICE. *Ta-da!*

THE HUSBAND. Like it was a flag, unfurled.

THE PSYCHIATRIST. Many women — following confirmation of their pregnancy — experience a depressive lull, and — subsequently — guilt over their lack of elation. But not Alice.

ALICE. I had too much to do! I had to prepare … life's ultimate exam … isn't that a baby? Isn't that *raising a child?*

THE HUSBAND. We bought books. We started downloading. We called friends, friends with children, friends with newborns. We took Lamaze. *(Together — grinning ear to ear — Alice and her husband demonstrate their breathing technique. All the oxygen makes Alice's husband dizzy.)*

ALICE. I read Dr. Spock. Even Piaget. I read all about colostrum, and myelination, and the evolution of motor skills, and object permanence. I don't think it would be unfair to suggest — to state, even — that I knew what to expect.

THE PSYCHIATRIST. Needless to say, Alice was … surprised … when the baby began to — to — *(The Psychiatrist seeks the appropriate word. He turns to Alice for confirmation:)* — vocalize? — *(Alice nods.)* — while still inside the womb. *(Alice places a hand on her belly.)*

ALICE. I knew I'd feel things. Flutters. Kicks. But sounds? *(Lights rise on an actor on another, higher stool. He has the sexy, slightly slouchy look of a studio musician. He clutches a microphone. He portrays the*

Baby. Right now, he coos — ever so softly — into the mike, then accentuates it with a tiny rippling sound. In an enthusiastic whisper:) Shhhh! Quiet, and you'll hear. I'm not teasing. I'm not making this up. Oh! There it goes! *(Alice positively squirms with pleasure. The Psychiatrist consults his clipboard; he quotes Alice.)*

THE PSYCHIATRIST. "The sort of sounds that might" — and here you'll note that Alice is quite specific, quite vivid — "that might *issue from the bottom of the ocean floor.*"

ALICE. Soothing. Like those tapes you buy of rainstorms, or the lapping of waves.

THE PSYCHIATRIST. Soon, however, the sounds hardened into consonants. *(Alice lifts her blouse; her belly undulates with the baby's first effort at actual speech.)*

THE BABY. Mmmmmm … fffffffff … shhhhhhh … Kah. Kah. Duh. Duh. Duh.

ALICE. *(Delighted.)* Syncopation!

THE PSYCHIATRIST. Syllables followed, not long after.

THE BABY. Bah. Fah. Pah. Hom. Ling.

THE PSYCHIATRIST. In my encounters with Alice, I tried to suggest — delicately, of course — that the sounds were organic in nature. Gastrointestinal.

ALICE. And I told him to find a stethoscope — like a *proper doctor* — and put it over my womb.

THE PSYCHIATRIST. She was insistent, just the same.

ALICE. I told him he'd hear *scales. (The Baby sings a scale.)* His first word in-utero. I'll never forget it:

THE BABY. Conundrum. *(The Psychiatrist smiles at Alice, then offers:)*

THE PSYCHIATRIST. An ambitious word. More sophisticated than one would expect.

ALICE. I'd lie on my back, and drape my hands over my belly. I'd hear them in my sleep.

THE BABY. Free-fall. Sartorial. Quaff.

ALICE. When I woke up, I'd write them down. Half the time, I had to consult a dictionary. "Quaff"?

THE BABY. "To drink deeply. To drain. To take long draughts."

ALICE. Why, yes. Of course. "Quaff." Q-U-A-F-F. "Quaff."

THE HUSBAND. The first strange behavior I noticed was her

speech. I'd come home from work, I'd be having a beer —

ALICE. *(To her husband.)* Darling! Don't *quaff* that *libation.*

THE HUSBAND. Alice is articulate, sure, but she isn't a wordsmith, she isn't a —

THE BABY. Lexicographer?

THE HUSBAND. — yet here she was, talking like a goddamn spelling bee.

ALICE. My vocabulary grew by leaps and bounds.

THE PSYCHIATRIST. By its fifth month, the child was composing sentences.

ALICE. With most babies, it's "Gimme wa-wa" or "Baby hafta poo."

THE PSYCHIATRIST. But instead, the child opted for a loftier tone. *(The Baby speaks in a thrilling baritone:)*

THE BABY. "When wintry branches scrape the sky, on midnight steed Death gallops by!"

THE PSYCHIATRIST. Alice marveled at her baby's verse. *(Alice clutches her stomach in wonder and cries:)*

ALICE. Again! Oh, say it again!

THE BABY. *(Reading to Alice, as if curled up by the fire:)* "Happy families are all alike, but every unhappy family is unhappy in its own way … "

THE PSYCHIATRIST. Elegiac as it was, it gave her a strange comfort.

ALICE. I worried I might be crazy. Hearing voices. I know that's not normal; I know that's not right.

THE PSYCHIATRIST. But she soon put these fears to rest. After all, the content of the child's musings was beyond her.

ALICE. I've never been much of a reader myself. And I certainly don't compose poetry; I couldn't even rhyme "spoon."

THE BABY. Loon. Moon. June. Festoon. Harpoon. Macaroon. Sasquetoon.

THE PSYCHIATRIST. With the devotion of an acolyte, Alice began to take dictation from the child.

THE HUSBAND. The notebooks. That was my next clue. Three of 'em, spiral-bound. One was full of poetry. The second was anagrams —

THE BABY. Dog. God!

THE HUSBAND. — that kinda thing. And the last … the last

was gibberish. *(Alice shoots a glare at her husband.)*

ALICE. Eastern philosophy, mostly. *(The Baby intones a sacred Buddhist chant, his voice rising to a mesmerizing pitch; Alice — in ecstasy — raises her palms heavenward. She is bathed in a mystical light.)* We'd planned on raising our child Presbyterian; now I wasn't so sure.

THE PSYCHIATRIST. Soon, the child's fascination with language waned; it opted instead for pragmatism.

THE BABY. *(Rapid-fire, tough.)* And it's High-Tone on the outside, on the outside, Shenandoah in third place ... and Musket Fire's pulling ahead ... pulling ahead ... taking the lead! Musket Fire's in the lead! *(A pause. All three characters glance at one another for a moment, then Alice turns full-out again and whispers:)*

ALICE. The ponies; it's true!

THE PSYCHIATRIST. Alice would drape the racing forms about her mid-section, and in her ear the infant would coo:

THE BABY. *(A whispered tip:)* Lucky Lady in the Third Lap ... Ten down on Strawberry Fields ...

THE PSYCHIATRIST. Alice, who had never before demonstrated an interest in the track, soon found herself spending long afternoons at QTB.

ALICE. I used my winnings to buy a wicker bassinet and a hand-sewn collection of antique baby quilts. *(Once again, Alice glances at her husband:)* Our child was the beneficiary; *not me.*

THE PSYCHIATRIST. In the kitchen, she would open *The Joy of Cooking*, and slip it under her elastic waistband. While she puttered amidst mixing bowls and measuring cups, the baby would recite the recipe.

THE BABY. *(A French chef:)* That is the miracle of the phyllo pastry; it is densely layered, but it still has a light texture.

ALICE. Once, we made bulgur pilaf. Another time — mmm! — *fennel puree.*

THE PSYCHIATRIST. Sometimes, the child would insist —

THE BABY. Another dollop of creme de cacao!

THE PSYCHIATRIST. — or —

THE BABY. Why so stingy with the coriander?

THE HUSBAND. All pregnant women have cravings, right? Only instead of pickles, my wife wanted foie gras and escargot.

THE PSYCHIATRIST. Many theoreticians believe that mother-child communication begins prenatally. Many women sing to their unborn children; others rock or coo, and report intra-uterine response. Still — by any standard — Alice's interaction with her fetus exceeded the norm.

THE BABY. *(A* Town & Country *tennis instructor:)* Step and hit ... step and hit ... step and hit! *(Approvingly:)* Killer back-hand, Alice!

ALICE. I've always been a loner. Every morning, my husband would go to work, and there I'd be. In the house. Like a rat in a Skinner box, sniffing the walls. So it was nice. It was nice to have someone there, with me. To do things.

THE BABY. Checkmate.

ALICE. Sometimes, he'd let me win. Just to buoy my confidence.

THE BABY. Sixteen across: What's an eight letter word that means *hyperbole?*

ALICE. Some women complain about the third trimester; not me. The days flew.

THE BABY. *(The slacker frat-boy:)* Right hand, red. Left foot, green. I'm gonna spin it now. I'm gonna spin it ... Left hand, yellow. Right foot, blue!

ALICE. Around the seventh month, his tone changed. It ... ah ... *deepened. (The Baby swigs Scotch from a flask.)*

THE BABY. *(The seducer:)* I like you in the red dress better. *(A pause. Alice digests this.)*

ALICE. Frankly, it was nice to know that he had preferences.

THE BABY. Why, Alice. You cut your hair.

ALICE. He noticed.

THE BABY. *(Low, sensual:)* You're wearing them tonight, aren't you? Aren't you? The silk panties with the ecru lace? *(Alice blushes. The Baby holds the mike close to his mouth and gives a tiny blow, as if he were cooling a pie. Again. And again. Each time he blows, Alice gives a sharp cry of delight. This lasts for some time, until Alice has a toe-curling orgasm.)*

THE HUSBAND. I felt shut out. Like I didn't exist anymore. *(The Baby takes out a cigarette, lights it, and begins to smoke.)*

ALICE. I became complacent; that's the problem. I began to expect happiness. Not as an end result; not as a goal. As a state of being.

THE PSYCHIATRIST. It wasn't until the eighth month that the

fetus became impertinent.

ALICE. It came out of the blue.

THE BABY. *(Simply:)* Cunt. *(A silence. The word hangs heavy in the air, like a toxin.)*

ALICE. It was … it was a wrecking ball in the back of my head. And it only got worse. *(The Baby's voice turns low and malevolent.)*

THE BABY. Bitch. Gash. *Pod.*

ALICE. I'd jolt awake in the middle of the night. I'd be sweating into my pillow. It would hiss. Hiss at me. *(The Baby chants in a wicked, singsong rhythm:)*

THE BABY. Water weight, water weight, water weight … *(Alice flinches at each repetition of the words. Soon, she's chanting along with the child, her voice tremulous with fear:)*

ALICE. Water weight, water weight, water weight …

THE PSYCHIATRIST. Her husband would roll over and moan —

THE HUSBAND. Honey? Is that you?

THE PSYCHIATRIST. — and Alice would be forced to bite her tongue.

ALICE. I couldn't tell him. How could I tell him?

THE HUSBAND. She pulled up inside herself and stayed there.

THE PSYCHIATRIST. By the ninth month, the child had turned insidious.

THE BABY. Remember those foot braces you wore as a baby? Clunk, clunk, clunk against the sides of your crib … *(The Baby slams his Scotch glass against the live mike, to duplicate the sound. Alice nods with recognition and dread.)*

THE BABY. Well, wait'll you see me. I've got webbed toes and a purple rash. *(Alice gives a tiny cry of horror.)*

THE PSYCHIATRIST. Finally, the infant went too far. It began to catalogue its own deformities with disconcerting relish.

THE BABY. Spina bifida!

ALICE. *(Terrified now:)* Oh, God.

THE BABY. Hydrocephalus.

ALICE. No!

THE BABY. Dwarfism!

ALICE. No, no, no — I saw the sonograms, I saw them myself —

THE BABY. DOWN'S SYNDROME!

ALICE. Each little finger, each little toe —

THE BABY. You'll have to enroll me in ... sp ... sp ... sp ... SPECIAL classes, and physical therapy, and — once a week or so — *cranial drainage* —

ALICE. I don't have the strength, I don't have the patience —

THE BABY. — pushing me down the aisle of Toys 'R' Us in my motorized stroller with the tubes and the fibrulator —

ALICE. *(A desperate protest:)* I AM NOT GOOD! I AM NOT SELFLESS!

THE BABY. *(With Satanic reverb:)* YOU'RE CONDEMNED TO LOVE ME, REGARDLESS —

THE PSYCHIATRIST. — the child told her —

THE BABY. — EVEN IF I'VE A FORKED TONGUE AND A TAIL!!!! *(In a hushed whisper, Alice starts to utter the Lord's prayer.)*

ALICE. Our Father who art in Heaven, hallowed be thy name ...

THE HUSBAND. I was in the garage, just futzing around, seeking a little *peace*, and in she came. She asked me ... our child, the one we'd worked so hard to conceive ... *she actually asked me ... (Alice raises a knitting needle. She stares at her husband imploringly. He turns abruptly away. It's too awful to contemplate.)* I told her it was too late. That it wouldn't be *legal*.

ALICE. *(In a tiny voice:)* I was afraid. I was. So. Afraid.

THE PSYCHIATRIST. Alice's fear soon gave way to anger. Her rage began to grow along with the child.

ALICE. I was its room, I was its board, I was its future. How could it ... How dare it ...

THE PSYCHIATRIST. She began to count the days until her due date.

THE HUSBAND. She went from lying around all day in a stupor —

THE PSYCHIATRIST. — despondency —

THE HUSBAND. — to bouncing around the house like a goddamn pinball.

THE PSYCHIATRIST. — hypomania.

ALICE. I didn't want to birth it; no. I wanted to expel it.

THE HUSBAND. I'd never seen anything like it; hormones, I thought.

ALICE. I wanted to purge it from my body. But most of all ... I wanted to confront it, face to face. *(Alice turns to stare at The Baby.*

He shoots a glare right back at her. They gird themselves for the final battle.)

THE PSYCHIATRIST. The day finally arrived. The labor was grueling.

THE HUSBAND. Alice cursed a blue streak.

ALICE. *It wasn't my voice they heard!*

THE BABY. I'M NOT FUCKING LEAVING! SQUATTER'S RIGHTS!

THE HUSBAND. I was embarrassed to tell you the truth.

THE BABY. YOU PACK UP YOUR FRIGGING FORCEPS, BONE-MAN, AND YOU GET THE HELL OUTTA MY MAMA'S PRIVATES!

THE HUSBAND. You figure the nurses — they've seen it all, right? — and even they were shocked.

THE BABY. I GOT HER BY THE KIDNEY — I GOT HER BY THE BOWELS — AND I AIN'T GONNA FUCKIN' LET GO —

THE HUSBAND. Then I saw its head crown.

THE PSYCHIATRIST. Seven pounds, six ounces. Twenty-one inches long. Blue eyes, with the palest tufts of blonde hair. *(The Husband chokes up; he takes a moment to compose himself.)*

THE HUSBAND. In spite of everything — at that moment — I couldn't help it. I loved her. Fiercely.

THE PSYCHIATRIST. The doctors bathed the baby, and soon delivered a small, pink bundle into Alice's arms. *(Alice raises her arm, as if holding the baby.)* It lay there, wrinkled, its blurry eyes exhausted from the rigors of birth.

ALICE. *(Belligerent.)* Well? What do you have to say for yourself now?

THE PSYCHIATRIST. Alice was hardly prepared for the silence which followed. *(The actor portraying The Baby shuts off his microphone and unplugs the cord, which drops limply on the floor. He exits the stage. His footfalls continues in the wings, until we hear a distant door slam, and he is truly gone.)*

ALICE. It clammed up. It just lay there.

THE PSYCHIATRIST. It squirmed and it drooled, but it didn't say a word. It could cry full-throttle and later — after a few months — it would babble, but as for grand pronouncements and poetry readings, well, there were none.

ALICE. It was, I think, the final betrayal.

THE PSYCHIATRIST. Alice refused to hold the child; she refused to nurse it.

ALICE. Would you?

THE HUSBAND. What could I do? I had said to myself — I don't know how many times — "for the sake of the baby." We'll stick this out. We'll work this through. But I had to face facts. *(Alice and her husband exchange a lingering look, ripe with recriminations and unspoken argument. Then he breaks the stare.)* That logic, it just wasn't paying off.

THE PSYCHIATRIST. Alice's husband was — understandably — quite upset. He wanted some confirmation that his feelings — his own fury — wasn't misplaced.

THE HUSBAND. *(To the Psychiatrist:)* I'm seeking custody, Doc. And I want you to testify at the hearing.

THE PSYCHIATRIST. I took a hard line. Borderline. Psychotic. These are the words I chose.

THE HUSBAND. You don't pull punches. Not where your kids are concerned.

THE PSYCHIATRIST. Against our recommendation, the court granted Alice visitation privileges. *(The Psychiatrist exchanges a concerned glance with the Husband.)* Twice a week. *(And another.)* Unsupervised.

ALICE. I'm a patient person; I can wait.

THE PSYCHIATRIST. Her husband calls me to report that Alice is distant with the child — unresponsive — but not actively harmful.

THE HUSBAND. She looks at it, mostly. Like she's expecting something. Like it's a seed, waiting to sprout, and if she stares — long enough, and hard enough — it'll grow.

ALICE. It's a battle of wills, that's all. But one day, it will happen. It will crack open its little maw. It'll use its tongue to shape poison arrows. It will begin innocently enough, I'm sure. *(She casts a look at her husband.)* "Da-da." *(Then at the Psychiatrist.)* "Boo-Boo." But the rest will follow soon enough. *(She returns to her knitting with quiet vigor. In her voice, a calm certainty. So certain it's chilling.)* It might take months. It might take years. But — in the end

— vengeance will be mine. *(Suddenly — unexpectedly — the happy gurgling of a child. Alice's eyebrow cocks. She listens. It has begun. She coos back at the infant; it giggles. Soon, Mother and child are engaged in a nursery-time call-and-response. Blackout.)*

The End

PROPERTY LIST

UNWRAP YOUR CANDY (PART ONE)
Ticket stub (PHYSICIAN)
Coat (PHYSICIAN)
Playbill (PHYSICIAN)
Purse (FASHIONABLE WOMAN)
Wrapped piece of candy (FASHIONABLE WOMAN)
Cell phone (GABBY LADY)
Infrared headset (FASHIONABLE WOMAN)
Beeper (PHYSICIAN)

LOT 13: THE BONE VIOLIN
Gavel (AUCTIONEER)
Small coffin (AUCTIONEER)
Concert program (MOTHER)

WILDWOOD PARK
Folded newspaper (DR. SIMIAN)
Sunglasses (MS. HAVILAND, DR. SIMIAN)
Business card (MS. HAVILAND)

BABY TALK
Cigarette and lighter/matches
Knitting needles and yam (MOTHER)
Microphone (BABY)
Clipboard (PSYCHIATRIST)
Flask (BABY)
Glass of Scotch (BABY)
Knitting needle (ALICE)

SOUND EFFECTS

UNWRAP YOUR CANDY (PART ONE)
Crash-boxes tumbling over in a heap
Amplified sound of candy wrapper crinkling
Cell phones ringing
Beepers
Snoring
Sighs
People shifting in seats
Gastrointestinal rumblings

LOT 13: THE BONE VIOLIN
Orchestra tuning
Audience settling before a concert
Few notes of *Peter and the Wolf*
Three versions of Beethoven's *Sonata Number Eight*
Tchaikovsky's *Melancholique*
Tick-tock of a clock
Piercing sound of note played incorrectly on a violin
Paganini's *Rondo*

WILDWOOD PARK
Children playing

UNWRAP YOUR CANDY (PART THREE)
Exchange with a cabbie
Car horn

BABY TALK
A child gurgling

NEW PLAYS

★ **MONTHS ON END by Craig Pospisil.** In comic scenes, one for each month of the year, we follow the intertwined worlds of a circle of friends and family whose lives are poised between happiness and heartbreak. "...a triumph...these twelve vignettes all form crucial pieces in the eternal puzzle known as human relationships, an area in which the playwright displays an assured knowledge that spans deep sorrow to unbounded happiness." –*Ann Arbor News.* "...rings with emotional truth, humor...[an] endearing contemplation on love...entertaining and satisfying." –*Oakland Press.* [5M, 5W] ISBN: 0-8222-1892-5

★ **GOOD THING by Jessica Goldberg.** Brings us into the households of John and Nancy Roy, forty-something high-school guidance counselors whose marriage has been increasingly on the rocks and Dean and Mary, recent graduates struggling to make their way in life. "...a blend of gritty social drama, poetic humor and unsubtle existential contemplation..." –*Variety.* [3M, 3W] ISBN: 0-8222-1869-0

★ **THE DEAD EYE BOY by Angus MacLachlan.** Having fallen in love at their Narcotics Anonymous meeting, Billy and Shirley-Diane are striving to overcome the past together. But their relationship is complicated by the presence of Sorin, Shirley-Diane's fourteen-year-old son, a damaged reminder of her dark past. "...a grim, insightful portrait of an unmoored family..." –*NY Times.* "MacLachlan's play isn't for the squeamish, but then, tragic stories delivered at such an unrelenting fever pitch rarely are." –*Variety.* [1M, 1W, 1 boy] ISBN: 0-8222-1844-5

★ **[SIC] by Melissa James Gibson.** In adjacent apartments three young, ambitious neighbors come together to discuss, flirt, argue, share their dreams and plan their futures with unequal degrees of deep hopefulness and abject despair. "A work...concerned with the sound and power of language..." –*NY Times.* "...a wonderfully original take on urban friendship and the comedy of manners—a *Design for Living* for our times..." –*NY Observer.* [3M, 2W] ISBN: 0-8222-1872-0

★ **LOOKING FOR NORMAL by Jane Anderson.** Roy and Irma's twenty-five-year marriage is thrown into turmoil when Roy confesses that he is actually a woman trapped in a man's body, forcing the couple to wrestle with the meaning of their marriage and the delicate dynamics of family. "Jane Anderson's bittersweet transgender domestic comedy-drama ...is thoughtful and touching and full of wit and wisdom. A real audience pleaser." –*Hollywood Reporter.* [5M, 4W] ISBN: 0-8222-1857-7

★ **ENDPAPERS by Thomas McCormack.** The regal Joshua Maynard, the old and ailing head of a mid-sized, family-owned book-publishing house in New York City, must name a successor. One faction in the house backs a smart, "pragmatic" manager, the other faction a smart, "sensitive" editor and both factions fear what the other's man could do to this house—and to them. "If Kaufman and Hart had undertaken a comedy about the publishing business, they might have written *Endpapers*...a breathlessly fast, funny, and thoughtful comedy ...keeps you amused, guessing, and often surprised...profound in its empathy for the paradoxes of human nature." –*NY Magazine.* [7M, 4W] ISBN: 0-8222-1908-5

★ **THE PAVILION by Craig Wright.** By turns poetic and comic, romantic and philosophical, this play asks old lovers to face the consequences of difficult choices made long ago. "The script's greatest strength lies in the genuineness of its feeling." –*Houston Chronicle.* "Wright's perceptive, gently witty writing makes this familiar situation fresh and thoroughly involving." –*Philadelphia Inquirer.* [2M, 1W (flexible casting)] ISBN: 0-8222-1898-4

DRAMATISTS PLAY SERVICE, INC.
440 Park Avenue South, New York, NY 10016 212-683-8960 Fax 212-213-1539
postmaster@dramatists.com www.dramatists.com

NEW PLAYS

★ **BE AGGRESSIVE by Annie Weisman.** Vista Del Sol is paradise, sandy beaches, avocado-lined streets. But for seventeen-year-old cheerleader Laura, everything changes when her mother is killed in a car crash, and she embarks on a journey to the Spirit Institute of the South where she can learn "cheer" with Bible belt intensity. "…filled with lingual gymnastics…stylized rapid-fire dialogue…" *–Variety.* "…a new, exciting, and unique voice in the American theatre…" *–BackStage West.* [1M, 4W, extras] ISBN: 0-8222-1894-1

★ **FOUR by Christopher Shinn.** Four people struggle desperately to connect in this quiet, sophisticated, moving drama. "…smart, broken-hearted…Mr. Shinn has a precocious and forgiving sense of how power shifts in the game of sexual pursuit…He promises to be a playwright to reckon with…" *–NY Times.* "A voice emerges from an American place. It's got humor, sadness and a fresh and touching rhythm that tell of the loneliness and secrets of life…[a] poetic, haunting play." *–NY Post.* [3M, 1W] ISBN: 0-8222-1850-X

★ **WONDER OF THE WORLD by David Lindsay-Abaire.** A madcap picaresque involving Niagara Falls, a lonely tour-boat captain, a pair of bickering private detectives and a husband's dirty little secret. "Exceedingly whimsical and playfully wicked. Winning and genial. A top-drawer production." *–NY Times.* "Full frontal lunacy is on display. A most assuredly fresh and hilarious tragicomedy of marital discord run amok…absolutely hysterical…" *–Variety.* [3M, 4W (doubling)] ISBN: 0-8222-1863-1

★ **QED by Peter Parnell.** Nobel Prize-winning physicist and all-around genius Richard Feynman holds forth with captivating wit and wisdom in this fascinating biographical play that originally starred Alan Alda. "QED is a seductive mix of science, human affections, moral courage, and comic eccentricity. It reflects on, among other things, death, the absence of God, travel to an unexplored country, the pleasures of drumming, and the need to know and understand." *–NY Magazine.* "Its rhythms correspond to the way that people—even geniuses—approach and avoid highly emotional issues, and it portrays Feynman with affection and awe." *–The New Yorker.* [1M, 1W] ISBN: 0-8222-1924-7

★ **UNWRAP YOUR CANDY by Doug Wright.** Alternately chilling and hilarious, this deliciously macabre collection of four bedtime tales for adults is guaranteed to keep you awake for nights on end. "Engaging and intellectually satisfying…a treat to watch." *–NY Times.* "Fiendishly clever. Mordantly funny and chilling. Doug Wright teases, freezes and zaps us." *–Village Voice.* "Four bite-size plays that bite back." *–Variety.* [flexible casting] ISBN: 0-8222-1871-2

★ **FURTHER THAN THE FURTHEST THING by Zinnie Harris.** On a remote island in the middle of the Atlantic secrets are buried. When the outside world comes calling, the islanders find their world blown apart from the inside as well as beyond. "Harris winningly produces an intimate and poetic, as well as political, family saga." *–Independent (London).* "Harris' enthralling adventure of a play marks a departure from stale, well-furrowed theatrical terrain." *–Evening Standard (London).* [3M, 2W] ISBN: 0-8222-1874-7

★ **THE DESIGNATED MOURNER by Wallace Shawn.** The story of three people living in a country where what sort of books people like to read and how they choose to amuse themselves becomes both firmly personal and unexpectedly entangled with questions of survival. "This is a playwright who does not just tell you what it is like to be arrested at night by goons or to fall morally apart and become an aimless yet weirdly contented ghost yourself. He has the originality to make you feel it." *–Times (London).* "A fascinating play with beautiful passages of writing…" *–Variety.* [2M, 1W] ISBN: 0-8222-1848-8

DRAMATISTS PLAY SERVICE, INC.
440 Park Avenue South, New York, NY 10016 212-683-8960 Fax 212-213-1539
postmaster@dramatists.com www.dramatists.com

NEW PLAYS

★ **SHEL'S SHORTS by Shel Silverstein.** Lauded poet, songwriter and author of children's books, the incomparable Shel Silverstein's short plays are deeply infused with the same wicked sense of humor that made him famous. "…[a] childlike honesty and twisted sense of humor." *–Boston Herald.* "…terse dialogue and an absurdity laced with a tang of dread give [*Shel's Shorts*] more than a trace of Samuel Beckett's comic existentialism." *–Boston Phoenix.* [flexible casting] ISBN: 0-8222-1897-6

★ **AN ADULT EVENING OF SHEL SILVERSTEIN by Shel Silverstein.** Welcome to the darkly comic world of Shel Silverstein, a world where nothing is as it seems and where the most innocent conversation can turn menacing in an instant. These ten imaginative plays vary widely in content, but the style is unmistakable. "…[*An Adult Evening*] shows off Silverstein's virtuosic gift for wordplay…[and] sends the audience out…with a clear appreciation of human nature as perverse and laughable." *–NY Times.* [flexible casting] ISBN: 0-8222-1873-9

★ **WHERE'S MY MONEY? by John Patrick Shanley.** A caustic and sardonic vivisection of the institution of marriage, laced with the author's inimitable razor-sharp wit. "…Shanley's gift for acid-laced one-liners and emotionally tumescent exchanges is certainly potent…" *–Variety.* "…lively, smart, occasionally scary and rich in reverse wisdom." *–NY Times.* [3M, 3W] ISBN: 0-8222-1865-8

★ **A FEW STOUT INDIVIDUALS by John Guare.** A wonderfully screwy comedy-drama that figures Ulysses S. Grant in the throes of writing his memoirs, surrounded by a cast of fantastical characters, including the Emperor and Empress of Japan, the opera star Adelina Patti and Mark Twain. "Guare's smarts, passion and creativity skyrocket to awesome heights…" *–Star Ledger.* "…precisely the kind of good new play that you might call an everyday miracle…every minute of it is fresh and newly alive…" *–Village Voice.* [10M, 3W] ISBN: 0-8222-1907-7

★ **BREATH, BOOM by Kia Corthron.** A look at fourteen years in the life of Prix, a Bronx native, from her ruthless girl-gang leadership at sixteen through her coming to maturity at thirty. "…vivid world, believable and eye-opening, a place worthy of a dramatic visit, where no one would want to live but many have to." *–NY Times.* "…rich with humor, terse vernacular strength and gritty detail…" *–Variety.* [1M, 9W] ISBN: 0-8222-1849-6

★ **THE LATE HENRY MOSS by Sam Shepard.** Two antagonistic brothers, Ray and Earl, are brought together after their father, Henry Moss, is found dead in his seedy New Mexico home in this classic Shepard tale. "…His singular gift has been for building mysteries out of the ordinary ingredients of American family life…" *–NY Times.* "…rich moments …Shepard finds gold." *–LA Times.* [7M, 1W] ISBN: 0-8222-1858-5

★ **THE CARPETBAGGER'S CHILDREN by Horton Foote.** One family's history spanning from the Civil War to WWII is recounted by three sisters in evocative, intertwining monologues. "…bittersweet music—[a] rhapsody of ambivalence…in its modest, garrulous way…theatrically daring." *–The New Yorker.* [3W] ISBN: 0-8222-1843-7

★ **THE NINA VARIATIONS by Steven Dietz.** In this funny, fierce and heartbreaking homage to *The Seagull*, Dietz puts Chekhov's star-crossed lovers in a room and doesn't let them out. "A perfect little jewel of a play…" *–Shepherdstown Chronicle.* "…a delightful revelation of a writer at play; and also an odd, haunting, moving theater piece of lingering beauty." *–Eastside Journal (Seattle).* [1M, 1W (flexible casting)] ISBN: 0-8222-1891-7

DRAMATISTS PLAY SERVICE, INC.
440 Park Avenue South, New York, NY 10016 212-683-8960 Fax 212-213-1539
postmaster@dramatists.com www.dramatists.com